When did the la

So

Presentation by *BookLeaf Publishing*

Web: www.bookleafpub.com

E-mail: info@bookleafpub.com

ISBN: 9789357616454

First edition 2022

To Mrs Swinnerton, who always said I was arty. It took my family (and me) until now to recognise it. To Mrs Crout, a wonderful teacher who gave me my love of Shakespeare and had a lot to do with my love of school.

ACKNOWLEDGEMENT

Despite having no editor, cover designer or publicist whose name I will ever know, there are some people who I should thank.

First, my parents, grandparents and dog. Second, my friends, both the ones I have kept in touch with and those who stopped answering my phone calls long ago.

Thirdly, my teachers - Mrs Crout and Mrs Swinnerton, whom I mentioned in my dedication; Mrs Godwin for help with poems and stories in the past; Mrs Foster for her weekly Wednesday inspirations that led to some really strange poems (none of which are in this book); all my tutors, even the ones who don't teach me English (which is obviously most of you); all the other teachers I've had in the past who I haven't explicitly mentioned here; my singing teacher, Joanne, and my piano teacher, Dellal, who have kept teaching me through babies, covid and semi-retirement respectively; and to Simon, who is an amazing sight-reader and has accompanied me at National Trust Houses so many times I've lost count. Thanks also to William Gallagher, who is sort-of-almost-but-not-really a teacher, and the other writers at Spark Young Writers club, especially the ones who are just as morbid as me (I will never forget Mr Smith the lorry-driving alien!). "Voices" was written in one of those sessions.

I suppose I should thank Those Who Shall Not Be Named In Any Publication With My Name On The

Cover, for giving me enough sadness and anger to write poems like these on death, loneliness and other issues. But I'm not willing to thank them for anything because they ruined so many lives, so they can go gratitude-less and lonely into oblivion. I hope they see my name on this book and (if I ever actually finish a novel) others in the future and realise that though they did their best to squash it, the AB spirit goes on forever.

Thanks also to people who actually bought this book without knowing me, and to those readers who do know me. I have a terrible habit of reading acknowledgements before reading the book, so this is without the assumption that you (whoever you are) went through the entire thing before getting to this, because I don't want to make you feel guilty about reading the acknowledgements first by saying 'thanks for reading'. I hope you enjoy/enjoyed it, or were at least emotionally affected, which, as in the blurb, is the entire point. If you read all eighteen poems and didn't feel anything at all, we may be closer to the world described in "Unrequited" than I thought, but it won't matter to you anyway.

It feels necessary to thank the authors of every book I've ever read, because it's all influenced or inspired me in some way, whether to poetry, prose or doodles on my very messy and increasingly ripped desk pad.

Finally, thank you to anyone I haven't mentioned who was at any point involved in my life in a meaningful way that could possibly have affected my creativity.

Stars

The stars in silence singing to the moon,
Who winks and sparkles back at them,
Receding from the sky.

Ethereal light in the midst of blue.
A cold, dark night with hope shining through
As the bright stars glow.

Like lanterns in a dark, cold room;
Or a silver glint in a pile of lead,
They guide us to the truth.

We know that they're just balls of burning gas,
Explained to us by science alone:
But still, we dream.

Poison

Silent mists and stealthy fogs,
They creep into your lungs,
Pollute your breath, the very air you breathe,
And weigh you down.
Turn your heart to something heavy and cold,
An entity which lives inside of you
And is now flawed.

The poison spreads.
From heart, to blood, to head,
It spreads its murk and filth
Until your very soul is eaten up,
And you are just a shell of what you were.

Do you know what they are?
These things, these silent mists and stealthy fogs that leak
their poison all through you,
Do you know what they are yet?
Here's one final clue:

They seep in:
Ears then head then heart.
Then soul.
Devour your essence and wear you down to nothing,
worthless, empty.
You believe it.
Mistake. That is what they hoped for.
That is what they wanted all along.

Haunting

The wind is howling and the rain is freezing,
And an owl hoots in the branches above.
The moon glimmers white in the black-as-death sky,
And the leaves hiss a whisper as they twist and turn.

The castle sits high on the hillside before us,
Towers and turrets and ancient stone.
History in the woodwork; ghouls in the bones.

Hundreds of deaths and murders and killings;
A poisoned Archbishop and the stabbed Prince of Rome.
All their spirits floating freely
In that castle they call home.

No-one from nearby will go
Near the castle after dark.
They say people have seen ghostly figures around,
That the dead are their ancestors who never slept sound.

But tonight we are brave and tonight we are bold.
We will go in and prove it by not making a sound.
And the howls and the whispers, the hoot and the glow,
They don't scare us at all – let me show you around…

Loneliness

Trapped in a cage of glass,
That is seems there are no walls, but there are.
And there's no way out, however hard you try.

The day grows old, gives way to night.
The night grows old, gives way to day.
And though the outside world is seen,
The glass walls are still there.

Everywhere around you, life goes on,
And though you try, you can't quite reach them all.
For you can hear, and see, and smell, and sense,
But you are here, and they –
They are there.

The glass-walled cage, you know, does not exist.
Or it is only in your mind, at least,
Thick bars of separation
That even when you touch you still can't reach
Another person:
You're all alone, though you're surrounded.

Invisible

"Invisible" is a word that reeks
Of intrigue, of mystery.
Things unseen,
Disguised or hidden.

A person is invisible
When they're lost in a crowd.
Grouped together, mingling,
Not seen even if they shout out loud.

Spoken secrets are invisible,
Not tangible
Or physical;
Drifting minute waves upon the air.

People are invisible
When taken from the world.
Locked away or dead in the ground:
Unseen, unnoticed, rarely missed.

Or is "invisible" just a state of mind?
Do we choose what we see, what we hear or find?
Perhaps we do.
Perhaps "invisible" is just something left behind.

Snowdrops

A field of raised white heads
That gaze up with us at the stars.
Dew collecting, glinting faintly
As morning now draws near.

Bell-like flowers, their noise would be a spirit's laugh,
A quiet tinkle of a mini-church's practice rings.
The pale flower that hangs, so sad, yet beauteous
Below the mirage-light of moon and stars.

As dawn creeps up, and birds begin to sing,
The sweet blooms droop,
Their faint scent the greatest perfume in the world,
And we can hear, just hear, the distant ring
Of bells, the pale flower's final call
Before the valley floods with sunlight.

The Breath

The house is dark,
the rooms in shades of black on grey
and grey on black.
Silhouette shapes,
impressions –
nothing more.

The silence is heavy,
that of a predator waiting,
not breathing.
Allowing a pause for the prey to turn,
exposing its neck,
its vulnerable throat.

My turn is slow
to look behind at the room before,
lost in darkness.

Shadow upon shadow,
black on grey and grey on black,
just vague dark shapes
and silence,
a predator holding its breath,
waiting for the turn
to expose my neck, my vulnerable throat.

Darkness.
Silence.
Waiting…

The light comes on.

Light and Dark

A dark silhouette against the star-scarred night sky,
Tall and imposing, proud.
The stars cluster high as it gazes on the world,
Giving this lightless figure a crown of stars.

Pinprick-World

A pinprick-world:
The land is broken; barren, worn.
Beads of blood collect instead of dew
Atop the rambling, ravaged pinprick-world of thorns.

Voices

You are alone,
Nothing and no-one nearby,
Certainly not within eyeshot or earshot.
You are completely alone.

It's peaceful, and quiet.
Just the birds and the snow,
Nothing else.
The fluffy white carpet a blanket,
Heavy and wet,
That sucks all the noise from the world.

You are alone with your thoughts, quiet an

Heat. Smoke. Light. I'm running, piece of paper balled up
in my hand, shoved into a back pocket, the pencil broken in
two on the floor.

The flames spread quicker than they ought, from the
next-door block of offices to these in mere seconds. The
fire escape route is choked up with tongues of them, and I
turn back, run the other way, the smoke sucked in with
every breath, each soot-stained gasp of impure air a little
harder than the last.

I can barely breathe.

I head for the window: the latch is jammed. My head is
fuzzy, my vision blurred. I throw a chair; the glass shatters,
tiny sparking diamonds raining down outside and in.

Flames curl around the doorframe, caress the wood,
leap, a shower of sparks, onto the desk.

I jump from the sill.

A smell, disinfectant I think, in the air; scratchy sheets and
bandaged hands, a plastic mask stuck to my face.

People died in that fire. I can sense it.

Their voices crept in with smoke, voices I recognise,
voices I don't:
You're lucky…
It should have been me to survive…
I want to go home, I am scared of the dark…
They talk in my head, natter and chatter, loud and
disturbing. Cruel.

When I'm recovered, I find my poem, unfinished, in the
pocket of the trousers I was wearing on that day.

I finish the poem, every word of it true.

You are alone with your thoughts, quiet and still,
And the whispers are there in your head,
Other thoughts that aren't really your own.

The whispers grow louder,
Increasing in volume and filling your brain.
It's not quiet anymore.
The whispers are there, always.
You are never really alone.

Mine

Behold the perfect pressed parchment
and the gold-nibbed pen.
Observe the ink drowned in darkness
and the words, thin shadow-webs.

See, the shelves, the secrets –
know that all you see is mine.

See, the shelves, the secrets –
know that all you know is mine.

Behold my perfect pressed parchment
and my gold-nibbed pen.
Observe my ink drowned in darkness
and my words, thin shadow-webs.

See the shelves, see the secrets –
and know that all you are…
is mine.

Living a Lie

Falsities, all of it.
Lies, every word.
Each sentence, each letter;
the sounds as I read it out loud.

Penned by a stranger.

I am not who I thought.
How can it be now that I discover it?
Why not before?
Why ever at all?

Everything has a reason, we're told,
but I don't see it.
I am a lie,
(nothing more, nothing less)
words from my soul in ink on the pages,
the diaried history of my existence, all written as though it
were true:
I never knew, honest.

I promise, I swear it.

If only I'd known then what I know now:
That I am a forgery.

Bruises

I dream that there's a better world out there:
It's warm and safe.
A place where school is school
and home is home;
A world where day is bright
and night is light, the nightmares banished.

I hope that's there's a better place somewhere,
where music floods the skies
and grass is evergreen;
The great oaks strong, their age unseen.

I pray that there's a kinder world out there.
One fine enough that every query
has an answer one can find.
Adventure has a taste there, happiness a scent.
Fantasy is real, the unknown here, beside me,
all around.
Where pens write worlds into being,
each one better than the last:
places you can really go; and you don't have to come back.

I dream that there's a better world out there;
someplace existence isn't heavy,
where sharp words heal instead of harm.
Where bruises, when they fade, are remembered fondly;
Even those that never fade,
the bruises on the heart.

Deaf

"Did you hear?
The newsboy's shouting,
the widow's crying,
the fishwives mutter and the pensioners stutter.
The gossip mill is turning,
the rumours grow unending.
The world will soon be changing,
did you hear?

"The story's growing bigger,
Howling children
screeching louder.
Everybody's talking, did you hear?
Did you hear?"

Point to chest, pull the air, uncross hands.
I. Did. Not.

It Is All

The sea is great and the sea is small.
I am the sea
and the sea is all.
The sea's all around me,
though I see the sea not.
I swim and I flounder,
I float and I fall.
The sea is a creature,
the sea, it's a thought.
It is living and breathing
and the sea is a corpse.
The sea is a woman
with a thousand high songs.
And the sea is man
who growls large,
whispers long.
The sea throws me up
and it pushes me down.
It tosses and turns
and it stops, ever still.
The sea, it is everything.
It holds Time,
Time pulls taut.
The sea is now and the sea is then.
The sea was once here
and I want to know when.
It is here now still,
though it never is seen.
For the sea, it is stealthy.

For the sea, it is all.

Deals with Death

The gossamer sheet between life and death,
A thin line that lies nowhere,
An in-between place
Where Life plays her games with Death.

The space in-between is a corridor, a hallway,
A place for one just to pass through.
From Life into Death
Is a short, short trip,
And it's a one-way road,
Always will be.

It only takes an instant to die.

From a living world to the land of the dead,
From the people of the present
To those stuck back in time.

The journey takes less than a blink of an eye.

And it shouldn't be reversible,
This move from one place to the next.

It's the way of Life.

It's the way of Death.

But there are people, people rare but in existence
Who can visit that void in-between.
The space between living and dying,
Where only Life and Death themselves
Should be seen.

It is there in that never-there emptiness,
In that gap where sense of time and place stops,
That these in-between people go to barter,
To broker deals between themselves and Death.

To save a life, and owe another in return.

I, Eye

At a certain time by the window,
A glance –
for what? To grasp a pencil, find the German dictionary to
check a word? It could be anything
– reveals something strange.
A vision, bold, distorted, magnified, somehow misshapen.

An eye, half in shadow, and half in the light.
Blue? Grey? Green?
Hard to tell.

Too-big curling lashes, expanded pupil;
pale outer wilderness,
a nothing landscape,
empty but for the bleached red veins like dry rivers.

The eye, immense, consuming.

It overlays vision, hides the desk
behind a semi-transparent veil.

Where are the pencils, the dictionary?
Ruler, notebooks, leaking pen all changed, wrought
curving, indistinct.
Hidden, behind the great blue-grey-green eye.
Just a glance, that was all.
A flicker of attention,
and now this:

A gelatinous, deformed monster.

The head jerks back.

It's gone.

A reflection.
Merely a reflection, grown from light and air in the lens of
the spectacles.
My own eye, reflected and refracted,
until it became the pupil of a dinosaur
peering through time.

Just my eye. My own eye.
But in the curving glass, that part of me became –
for just one glance, the briefest moment
– a monster.

Unrequited

It is the year three thousand and twenty-two; the people
have nothing.
Did we run out of tears?
Were there cries and wails once,
mournful songs of loss, grief, unrequited love?
What is love?
What would it be to feel it?

A thousand years ago, we're told,
there was artwork and music,
dancing and laughter.
When, I wonder, did the last laugh dance?
Did it fade in endless echoes through the years,
or was it there and then
– gone –
lost in an instant?

What is the sound of a laugh?

Once, there were poems, written from the heart.
A heart? What heart?
The heart is important, they say now.
It beats in your chest, keeps you alive.
Thud. Thud. Thud.
Pulse. Pulse. Pulse.

The beating shoes of dancers,
heads thrown back to the sky.
A funeral parade?
A thanks for good fortune?
None can tell.

Frenzied feet, quick, stamp, turn.
Love. Grief. Duty.
Fear. Hope. Ambition.
The feet beat, wild.
Listen; hear them. The heart.
Thud. Thud. Thud.
Beat. Beat. Beat.
Laugh – sob – laugh –

Silence.

Milton Keynes UK
Ingram Content Group UK Ltd.
UKHW020820251023
431306UK00016B/475

When did the last laugh dance?

Sophie Nock

BookLeaf
Publishing